Pebble™

Dogs

Dachshunds

by Lisa Trumbauer

Consulting Editor: Gail Saunders-Smith, PhD

Consultant: Jennifer Zablotny, DVM
Member, American Veterinary Medical Association

Capstone press
Mankato, Minnesota

Pebble Books are published by Capstone Press,
151 Good Counsel Drive, P.O. Box 669, Mankato, Minnesota 56002.
www.capstonepress.com

1 2 3 4 5 6 11 10 09 08 07 06

Library of Congress Cataloging-in-Publication Data
Trumbauer, Lisa, 1963–
    Dachshunds / by Lisa Trumbauer.
    p. cm.—(Pebble Books. Dogs)
    Summary: "Simple text and photographs present an introduction to the
dachshund breed, its growth from puppy to adult, and pet care information"—
Provided by publisher.
    Includes bibliographical references and index.
    ISBN-13: 978-0-7368-5332-3 (hardcover)
    ISBN-10: 0-7368-5332-4 (hardcover)
    1. Dachshunds—Juvenile literature. I. Title. II. Series.
SF429.D25T78 2006
636.753'8—dc22   2005021593

Note to Parents and Teachers

The Dogs set supports national science standards related to life
science. This book describes and illustrates dachshunds. The images
support early readers in understanding the text. The repetition of
words and phrases helps early readers learn new words. This book
also introduces early readers to subject-specific vocabulary words,
which are defined in the Glossary section. Early readers may need
assistance to read some words and to use the Table of Contents,
Glossary, Read More, Internet Sites, and Index sections of the book.

Table of Contents

4

Playful Dogs

Dachshunds are
small, playful dogs.
They have lots of energy.

Dachshunds like
to play in the dirt.
They dig to find animals
that live underground.

From Puppy to Adult

Newborn dachshunds cannot see or hear. Their eyes and ears open after about 10 days.

Dachshund puppies
look funny.
Their long noses and
floppy ears look too big.
Their legs are short.

Adult dachshunds
are small.
Their bodies are long
and thin like hot dogs.
Their legs are still short.

Dachshund Care

Dachshunds like
to run and dig.
They need exercise
to stay fit.

Dachshunds drink lots
of water after exercise.
Dog food gives them
energy to run and play.

Dachshunds with long
or wiry fur should be
brushed often.
Short-haired dachshunds
need sweaters
in cold weather.

Dachshunds like
to live with families.
Their owners should
play with them and
keep them safe.

Glossary

dig—to make a hole in the ground

energy—the ability to work and play for a long time without getting tired easily

exercise—physical activity and movement done to stay healthy

newborn—very young

playful—frisky and willing to play

wiry—tough and stiff

Read More

Kishel, Ann-Marie. *Dogs and Puppies.* First Step Nonfiction. Minneapolis: Lerner, 2006.

Stone, Lynn M. *Dachshunds.* Eye to Eye with Dogs. Vero Beach, Fla.: Rourke, 2003.

Internet Sites

FactHound offers a safe, fun way to find Internet sites related to this book. All of the sites on FactHound have been researched by our staff.

Here's how:

1. Visit *www.facthound.com*
2. Type in this special code **0736853324** for age-appropriate sites. Or enter a search word related to this book for a more general search.
3. Click on the **Fetch It** button.

FactHound will fetch the best sites for you!

Index

Word Count: 136
Grade: 1
Early-Intervention Level: 13

Editorial Credits
Martha E. H. Rustad, editor; Juliette Peters, designer; Jo Miller, photo researcher; Scott Thoms, photo editor

Photo Credits
Cheryl A. Ertelt, 4; Getty Images Inc./The Image Bank/Richard Drury, 12; Getty Images Inc./Photonica/Manzo Niikura, 14; Grant Heilman Photography/Myrleen Ferguson Cate, 20; Grant Heilman Photography/Robert Smith, 8; Kent Dannen, 10, 16; Mark Raycroft, cover; Nature Picture Library/Lynn M. Stone, 1; Norvia Behling, 6; Peter Arnold Inc./Klein, 18

DATE DUE		
SEP 1 9 2006	APR 1 2 2007	
SEP 2 0 2006	MAY 1 4 2007	
OCT 1 0 2006	MAY 2 1 2007	
OCT 1 9 2006	SEP 0 5 2007	
OCT 2 6 2006	SEP 1 7 2007	
NOV 0 9 2006		
NOV 2 9 2006	OCT 0 3 2007	
DEC 0 7 2006	NOV 1 6 2007	
DEC 2 0 2006	AUG 2 8 2008	
JAN 1 6 2007	SEP 2 3 2008	
JAN 2 4 2007	OCT 2 1 2008	
JAN 3 1 2007	AUG 2 6 2009	
FEB 1 9 2007		
FEB 2 8 2007		
MAR 0 9 2007		
MAR 1 2 2007		
MAR 2 1 2007		

HIGHSMITH 45